VINEYAR...
in Wessex and the West o...
by
Roger Crisp

Such is the prejudice of most people against anything of English growth, I generally find it most prudent not to declare where it grew, till after they had passed their verdict upon it.

DAVID GENESTE, *Vigneron,* c.1750

David Geneste was brought over from France by Sir Charles Hamilton to run his vineyard at Cobham in Surrey and the particular wine he was talking about was *oeil de Perdrix*, a champagne-style wine. English wines 250 years ago? Yes, and even that is only the recent history of vine growing in England.

An English vineyard in 1750

English wine has had a bad press in modern times. We've all come across 'country' wines at some time or another. In fact Britain appears to be the only place where wines are made from such diverse sources as tea, potatoes, elderberries and gooseberries, to name only a very few. But what of wine from grapes? The story of winemaking in Wessex is the story of winemaking throughout Britain.

The 'Musts' of time

In the known history of Britain there are only two periods when it seems that vines were *not* being grown here. The first is before the arrival of the Romans. Julius Caesar, in his writings of around 54 BC, made no mention of finding vines nor of winemaking anywhere in Britain. He would surely have noted the fact, since he took note of so much else. Wine was an important commodity in the Roman Empire at the time, being trusted more than any local water. The second period is between the two World Wars in the early part of the twentieth century.

When vines were not cultivated in Britain

Thus we can regard Britain as having a lot of its known history connected to the noble art of making wine from grapes. 'English wine is the real thing – and has been for 2,000 years', as Hugh Barty-King points out in his *A Taste of English Wine.* He goes on quite rightly to underline that 'English wine is not meant to be like a French or a German wine – it *is* English.'

English wine

SOMERSET VILLAGES
ENGLISH TABLE WINE
75cl   9.5%
1996
Medium Dry - Muller Thurgau
Grapes grown by Cannington College.
Wine made and bottled by Quantock Vineyards & Orchards,
The Counting House, Dodington, Somerset, UK

PRODUCE OF UNITED KINGDOM
W
VALLEY VINEYARDS
ASCOT
BRUT
QUALITY ENGLISH SPARKLING WINE
Traditional Method
11% vol   BOTTLED BY   VALLEY VINEYARDS RG10 0BN UK   75cl ℮

Two Thousand Years of English Wine

WHO AFTER WINE, TALKS OF WAR'S HARDSHIPS OR OF POVERTY?

The coming of the Romans

'Mumfords' was the old field-name for the land on which the Vineyard stands, recorded in ancient tithe maps and thought to be derived from 'Montfort'. Simon de Montfort owned land in the parish in 1250 AD. *The wine label has a Roman theme; near the vineyard are two Roman roads to Bath, and a Roman coin was found beneath a vine.*

It has always been presumed that the Romans brought the first vines with them. There is actually no written evidence of this, but we do know that some of their villas had their own vineyards. Roman terracing, suggesting the existence of vineyards, has been identified on the slopes around Corhampton (Hampshire, south-east Wessex) and near Basingstoke (Hampshire, north-east Wessex). Outside Wessex the definitive evidence comes from Wollaston, Northamptonshire, near Wellingborough (see *Current Archaeology* No 150). Wine was an integral part of their lifestyle and a great source of tax revenue for Rome. We do not know how far over Britain their vineyards extended, but, today, for example, there is a successful vineyard as far north as Durham.

Our evidence for the widespread practice of vinegrowing in Roman Britain is also through inference. In AD 81–96 the Emperor Domitian decreed that all planting of vineyards outside Italy must be halted, and also that all then existing ones outside Italy were to be halved. This ban seems to have been for two main reasons. First, this was through a concern that viticulture was being carried out as a 'cash crop' replacement for food crops, which would lead to food shortages and then rebellions. Second, and probably far more politically important, was that wine was taxed by price in Rome. This was a very lucrative means of making money. So, the Italian monopoly needed to be maintained keeping demand, prices and taxes high.

Our idea of the extent of vineyards in Britain comes two hundred years later, when, in AD 276, the Emperor Probus revoked the earlier decree and specifically mentioned Britain as a place where vinegrowing was to be allowed. Being an outpost of the Empire it is very likely that the previous ban had been poorly enforced in the first place and that the later decree from Probus was simply an admission of the actual state of affairs – that everyone was merrily growing their own vines regardless.

By the fifth century the Romans had little influence in Britain. With their departure it seems that viticulture declined. But it was not wiped out. There are at least three feasible reasons for this. The spread of Christianity accounts for two. First, it required wine for its ceremonies. Second, many monasteries were being created as the faith spread. Self-sufficiency was a very important goal of these establishments; they had the time and the patience to make the necessary research and experiments needed to prolong and revive viticulture. Third, and allied to the previous reason, was the fact that during the Dark Ages Britain was increasingly cut off, it seems, from continental trade and had to look after its own needs.

In that period, from AD 450–590 there was a succession of invasions along the east and south coasts by Jutes, Angles and Saxons. As with the Roman invasions the natives (by now Romano-British) would have been forced westwards, taking their vinegrowing techniques with them.

The Romans leave, the Saxons arrive

Background
Wylye Valley Vineyard

In Roman times Aust was a place of some importance, guarding the crossing of the Severn to Carleon and Caerwent. It is said that the good wine from the major vineyard nearby was sent back to Rome!. Aust's most famous visitor was Augustine, the first Archbishop of Canterbury, who met the unruly British (Welsh) Bishops on the banks of the Severn there.

SAINT AUGUSTINE'S VINEYARD

English Table Wine

11% Vol   **MM**   75cle

Bottled for Saint Augustine's Vineyard
Aust, Gloucestershire, United Kingdom
PRODUCE OF THE UNITED KINGDOM

Saxons and Normans

A carved panel in the choir-stalls of Winchester Cathedral showing a grape-vine.

The Normans – Christian invaders with a tradition of viticulture

The Saxons – who founded Wessex – regarded October as the 'Wyn Moneth' when the grape harvest was carried out. King Alfred recorded a law stating that any person found guilty of damaging another's field or vineyard would have to pay compensation. For such a statement to be made meant that Wessex still had a widespread tradition of viticulture. In 955 the Saxon King Edwy is recorded as giving a gift of a vineyard to the monks of Glastonbury. As we will see later the Glastonbury area of Somerset, at the heart of Wessex, is still a major winemaking area.

That wine and viticulture was a strong part of daily life can be traced in the actual word 'wine' itself. It meanders back through Old English, Old Frisian, Mid Lower German, Mid High German, to Old Norse where it means 'friend'. Also in Old English itself the word 'winemaez' means 'kinsman'.

Similarly, there is a theory that the city of Winchester derives its name from the same word. Under the Romans it seems that it was called 'Vintonia', then 'Wintonia' until the Saxon capital became Winchester. To corroborate this view even centuries later, John Twyne (writing in Latin) stated that 'It was called the City of Vine and Winegrowing stronghold and fortress where the best wine in Britain grew'. The poet Robert of Gloucester wrote (also in Latin), 'London is known for its shipping, Winchester for its wine'.

Although traumatic for the Saxons, the arrival of the Normans only enhanced the winemaking of Wessex and Britain. Being of the same religion meant that they did not destroy the monasteries, which were bastions of winemaking – and consumption. They established their own monasteries to add to the tradition. The Benedictine monks certainly knew how to market their expertise. They sold their produce to make good profits. Under royal assent they extended their influence and therefore their lands. The Norman castles likewise either consumed large quantities of wine or cultivated wine – or both. According to written accounts white wine was – as today – the most commonly produced type of wine, though for the religious communion a red colouring was necessary to fulfil the 'blood of Christ' requirement. Their churches and cathedrals have carvings of viticulture and wine making. The south transept of Wells Cathedral has carvings on the pillars, one such is a series, like a medieval cartoon story, depicting a farmer chasing two grape thieves. Thus, over the following 500 years, the vineyards of Wessex and Britain flourished.

THE TRADITION OF WINE GROWING AT BEAULIEU WAS ESTABLISHED BY CISTERCIAN MONKS WHO FOUNDED BEAULIEU ABBEY 1204. THE BEAULIEU ESTATE'S PRESENT VINEYARD WAS RE-ESTABLISHED BY COLONEL AND MRS GORE-BROWNE IN 1959, ON THE SAME SITE WHERE VINES WERE PLANTED BY JOHN DUKE OF MONTAGU IN 1735. THEN, MUCH OF THE WINE PRODUCED WAS DISTILLED FOR BRANDY; ONE SUCH BOTTLE, DATING FROM 1754, WAS FOUND IN THE WINE CELLAR IN PALACE HOUSE AS RECENTLY AS 1892!

2000

DRY WHITE

Produce of the United Kingdom

PRODUCED FROM GRAPES GROWN AT THE BEAULIEU ESTATE VINEYARD, HAMPSHIRE, UNITED KINGDOM. BOTTLED BY WICKHAM VINEYARDS, HAMPSHIRE, U.K.

THIS AWARD-WINNING W
PRODUCED MAINLY FRO
MÜLLER-THURGAU GRA
HAS A GOOD BALANCE OF
AND ACIDITY TO MAKE
AN IDEAL APERITIF O
ACCOMPANIMENT TO ANY
A TRADITIONAL-METHOD Q
SPARKLING WINE IS PROD
FROM THE SAME GRAP

12.5%vol 75cl

Compiled for William the Conqueror in 1086, the Domesday Book was also called the Winchester Roll because it was kept there for a time. We owe our first real verifiable evidence of the extent of vineyards in the country to the Normans. A total of 46 is listed in the 'Domesday Book'. Remember this is not a definitive list but a record for royal tax purposes. Nobody enjoys paying tax today, nor were things different then.

Missing from the list will be those vineyards owned by people who could afford to cook the books (or have it done for them) and many of the ecclesiastical vineyards were probably exempted from tax. Remember also that this is all in the context of a population of around 3 million people.

The 13th-century frieze in Salisbury Cathedral Chapter House – the Creation.

Some taxable Wessex vineyards listed in the 'Domesday Book'

Berkshire	Bisham	Bistesham: Henry de Ferrers. Church, vines.
Dorset	Durweston	Dervinestone/Derwinestone: Aiulf the Chamberlain; the wife of Hugh FitzGrip. Mill, vines.
	Wooton Fitzpaine	Odetun: Bretel from Count of Mortain; Aiulf the Chamberlain. 3 mills, vines.
Somerset	Glastonbury	Glastingberie/Glaestingeberia: Glastonbury Church. Vineyard. 5 cobs, 58 cattle, 20 pigs, 50 goats.
Wiltshire	Bradford on Avon	Bradeford: Abbess of Shaftesbury. 2 mills, market, vineyard. 1 sester of honey.

It seems probable that many vineyards were not included in the list of 46. If Winchester owed its name to wine, and the 'Domesday Book' was even kept there, we could reasonably expect some entries for that area. There are, in fact, no entries for Hampshire, meaning perhaps that many of the vineyards were already royal and therefore not taxed anyway. Cambridgeshire has only one entry at Ely, but the Normans themselves called it *L'Isle des Vignes*. Also, in the twelfth century, the historian William of Malmesbury, says 'No county has so many good vineyards as Gloucestershire', but only one, at Stonehouse, is listed decades earlier in the Book.

Little Ashley Vineyard is on the southernmost tip of the limestone Cotswolds overlooking the lovely old town of Bradford on Avon, with its Saxon Church, Medieval Tithe Barn and golden stone buildings. In 1086 the Domesday Book recorded a vineyard in the manor of Bradford. The cultivation was revived 900 years later when a new vineyard was planted in 1986 beside the 17th-century farmhouse at Little Ashley.

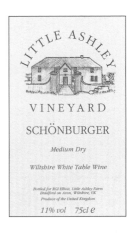

LITTLE ASHLEY

VINEYARD

SCHÖNBURGER

Medium Dry

Wiltshire White Table Wine

Bottled for RGI Elliott, Little Ashley Farm
Bradford on Avon, Wiltshire, UK
Produce of the United Kingdom

11% vol   75cl e

The first vineyard at Pilton, owned by Glastonbury Abbey, was in production before 1189 and the wine transported by barge to the Abbey. However, in 1260, the Abbot expanded his Deer Park and wine growing ceased for 700 years. The modern vineyard was first planted in 1966 on the same site and extends to 10.5 acres of Huxelrebe, Bacchus, Reichensteiner, Ortega, Seyval Blanc and Pinot Noir. The wines are made by the proprietor using new world techniques learned from top Australian winemaker John Worontschak.

At Avalon Vineyard the grapes are pressed in an adaptation of traditional, local technology. It is effective, appropriate and certainly very organic.

By 1155 the vineyard at Windsor Castle was producing wine 'to the king's profit'. And a Canterbury calendar for the year 1280/1 depicting monthly labours of the working man shows March as vine pruning, September as grape treading and January as, appropriately enough, wine drinking. Thus again we see how vinegrowing and winemaking were very much part of normal life.

The thirteenth-century historian, Bartholme, bears witness to the importance of Wessex, and Somerset in particular, in the skills and industry of viticulture. 'A good deal of Somerset must be land too fat and moist, in which the vine outrageth and beareth too many, too great and long leaves . . . and little fruit . . . [and yet] . . . the abbots of Glastonbury, who doubtless believed in the passing nobility of wine, than which nothing is more profitable if it be taken in due measure and manner, had vineyards on the sunny slopes of Pilton.' Wine in these times was usually drunk within a year. There was no easy way to store it. There were no glass bottles nor corks, and anything over a year old was referred to as 'old wine'.

During this first 300-year period of Norman rule in England much is often made of there having perhaps been a warmer climate, more favourable to vine cultivation than now. It has been recorded that around 1350 the Gulf Stream seems to have shifted its course, causing lower average temperatures. Roman times may also have been a period of relative warmth. Certainly we know that in the late Middle Ages, and after the Renaissance, winters became more severe. Whether climate is indeed a major problem for viticulture here in Wessex and the West of England is a moot point, but one which seems to be overridden by today's developments in Wessex especially, and in the country as a whole. As mentioned before, there is currently a vineyard in production as far north as Durham.

Perhaps far more influential was the coming of the Black Death, 1348–51, which wiped out more than half of England's four million population. Growing food of any kind would have been far more important than growing vines. Growing anything at all would have been difficult enough because of the lack of available labour and the abject fear of travelling to and from places for deliveries or collections. Vineyards would very much have been a preserve of the very well off who might have been able to insulate themselves from the effects of plague.

A major effect of the first and then subsequent plagues was that landowners were forced either to pay very high prices for labour (since it was at a premium) or put their land down for pasture. Many chose, or were forced, to do the latter. After all, it was much more cost effective to pay one shepherd rather than fifty labourers.

Indeed plague was to be a frequent visitor over the following 300 years, culminating in the *Annus Mirabilis*, as the poet John Dryden wrote, of 1666 when the Great Plague and the Great Fire of London occurred within twelve months of each other.

Perfectly ripe grapes hang heavy on the vine at Bagborough.

Wine, Monasteries and Dissolution

François Rabelais
Pantagruel, *1532*

Henry VIII and the Dissolution of the Monasteries

When Henry VIII came to power in 1509, 139 vineyards were recorded. Of these, 11 were royal vineyards, 67 belonged to the nobility and 52 were ecclesiastical. So, England was still a vinegrowing country. In 1586, William Camden, in his *Britannia*, had an opinion to offer on the 'climate theory' mentioned above. We are not to wonder that so many places in this country from their vines are called Vineyards, because they formerly afforded plenty of wine; and that they yield none now is rather to be imputed to the sloth of the inhabitants than the indisposition of the climate.'

From the survey at the start of Henry's reign, we can see that the Church still figured strongly in winemaking practices. Indeed, William Harrison wrote at the end of the century that the best English wine was ' "Theologicum", [as] it was from the clergy and religious men unto whose houses many of the laity would often send for bottles to be filled with the same.'

Although Henry dissolved many monasteries and their vineyards he widened the scope of the religious use of wine by ruling that the *whole* congregation, not just the clergy, should take wine at communion.

Wine had been coming from France in large quantities since 1154, when Henry II had married Eleanor of Aquitaine (the French Bordeaux wine area). For the thousand years before that Aquitaine had been sending wine to Britain ever since it had been part of Roman Gaul. Even a century before the Romans came the southern English (the Belgae) were known to have been importing wine from Europe. English wine had thus always survived because it was never really seen as being in competition with the French (or German) product. English wine had always been English and that was all there was to it.

So, although Henry wiped out the Roman Catholic Church, a ready source of foreign wine was still available. Wine drinking did not cease to be part of the English lifestyle. Vinegrowing itself was then kept going on a small scale by enthusiasts in country houses, and on an even smaller scale in gardens and south-facing house walls.

Small vineyard owners include those who run businesses unconnected with wine growing, are totally uncommercial, make wine for their own consumption, or sell wine in a small way.

LYTCHETT MATRAVERS
1998
SERVE CHILLED
10% vol.

SEYVAL BLANC
2001

Grapes grown and bottled at Carpenters Vineyard Norton sub Hamdon Somerset
75 cl   11% vol

Bed and Breakfast
for garden lovers

Friendly welcome with every comfort, and private bathroom. Well established garden with vineyard in lovely hamstone village.

2000
DURRA VALLEY
Schonburger
Medium Dry
Cornish Table Wine

2000

75cl   11%vol
Estate grown and bottled by Trevor Lockwood at Trezebel Cottage Manaccan Cornwall UK

Cufic
Müller Thurgau

Light Dry Table Wine
75cl. e   *from the Cheddar Valley* 10.5%vol.Alc.
Grown in the United Kingdom by Cufic Vines, Cheddar, Somerset Bottler W1271

ENGLISH RED TABLE WINE

11% Vol.   TRIOMPHE D'ALSACE   75cl.

produced and bottled by Mr & Mrs D. W. Carter at Rock Moors, Woodland Head, Crediton, Devon

The Art of the English Vineyard

Having pushed the actual growing of vines into small-scale hands, away from the huge previously ecclesiastical strongholds, Henry inadvertently turned the cultivation of vines into an art form. The practitioners of the art form became increasingly aware of their distinctive Englishness.

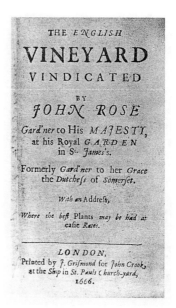

In 1666, John Rose, gardener to William III, wrote *The English Vineyard Vindicated*. He 'was the first to proclaim that English wine-grapes and English wine had a character and a tradition of their own' (Hugh Barty-King). Rose was writing four years *after* Christopher Merret gave his treatise on making 'wines sparkling'. This was 30 years *before* Dom Perignon is credited with popularizing champagne in France. He never claimed to have invented champagne, in fact he was intent on *stopping* the bubbles

The seventeenth century saw four important developments in the science of winemaking. The importing of cheap cane sugar, through the ports of Bristol and London, meant that sugar could cheaply – and effectively – be added to give a better balance to the wine (the process of chaptalisation). Also a test was developed for verifying the strength of the must (pressed grape juice). Today we do this with the hydrometer. In the seventeenth century a fresh egg did the trick. Honey, or sugar, was added until the egg floated just below the surface, 'to a depth of twopence', as Sir Kenelm

John Evelyn, Kalendarium Hortense 1670

January ...
If not finished set *Vines*, and begin to *prune* the *old*.

February ...
Plant *Vines* as yet.

June ...
You may now also (or in May before) cleanse *Vines* of exuberant *branches* and *tendrels*, cropping (not cutting) and stopping the second *joint* immediately before the *Fruit*, and some of the under branches which bear no *fruits*; especially in young *Vineyards* when they first begin to *bear*, and thence forwards; binding up the rest to *props*.

July ...
Towards the *later end*, visit your *Vineyards* again, etc. and *stop* the exuberant *shoots* at the *second joint* above the *fruit* (if not finished before); but not so as to expose it to the *Sun*, without some umbrage.

August ...
Continue yet to cleanse your *Vines* from exuberant *branches* that too much hinder the *Sun*.

September ...
Fruits in prime.

Little *Blew-grape*, *Muscadine grape*, *Frontiniac*, Parsley, great *Blew-grape*, the *Verjuice-grape* excellent for sauce, etc.

December ...
You may now plant *Vines*, etc.

Either late in this *month*, or in January, prune, and cut off all your *Vineshoots* to the very *root*, save *one* or *two* of the stoutest, to be left with three, or four *eyes* of *young wood*: This, for the *Vineyard*.

Wine in the Age of Reason

Galileo (1564–1642)

Beaulieu Abbey's medieval vineyard

Digby put it in 1669. The more sugar that was added the nearer the surface would come the egg. In England cork was being used to stop the *glass* bottle, allowing the wine to mature.

Experimentation was still important as viticulture moved into the eighteenth century. At Beaulieu Abbey Cistercian monks from France had begun to build the abbey in June, 1204. It had been completed by 1246. Its vineyard is presumed to have existed until Henry VIII's swingeing reforms, which affected the abbey in April 1588. There is actually no record of whether the vineyard survived or not. In 1736 John, 2nd Duke of Montagu, had the medieval vineyard replanted. Rather than make wine, though, he seems to have preferred to distill brandy. After his death the vineyard declined rapidly. There was a commercial vineyard at Claverton, near Bath, owned by Sir William Basset in 1743, according to *Notability of Bath*, 1871, by S. P. Major. During the eighteenth century the indoor growing of vines in glasshouses became fashionable.

Dr R. Worthington MD,
INVITATION TO THE
INHABITANTS OF ENGLAND
TO THE MANUFACTURE
OF WINES FROM THE
FRUITS OF THEIR OWN
COUNTRY, 1812.

I have myself proved that grapes caught by the frost will make sound wine. . . . There is more to be apprehended from foggy or wet weather than frost, but neither of them present any real objection against the establishment of vineyards in this kingdom. These existed and prospered centuries ago. . . . What therefore might not be hoped for under the present improved condition of natural science and horticulture?

In both the eighteenth and nineteenth centuries increasing numbers of books appeared on the subject of English wines. The optimism was premature. By 1834 the country's first case of powdery mildew had arrived. Then, in 1863, London had the distinction of reporting Europe's first case of phylloxera – a kind of vine louse. Ironically, the vines that had brought the phylloxera with them, when imported from America, were resistant to the insect, but local vines were not.

With viticulture not being on the same scale as in, say, France, the effects of disease were not as devastating as they might have been. The insect did not find it easy to transfer itself between disparate locations. As we have seen, English winemaking was alive and well but generally in the hands of small-scale, enthusiast operations throughout Wessex and southern England.

Any commercial side that did exist was, however, dealt another blow, at the same time as the disease factor presented itself. In 1860 the government, under Lord Palmerston (Liberal), drastically cut the tax on imported wines from 1s to 2d – a decrease of 83 per cent. Obviously the state's view of home grown wine as a source of valuable revenue had drastically changed from the time of Henry VIII.

The combined effect in Wessex of these developments was to discourage any expansion and to keep English wines in the backwaters of the agricultural scene. Land still had to be profitable to its owners before allowing the luxury of growing crops that were possibly uncommercial, and certainly unreliable, like wine grapes.

This twilight of the English winemaking tradition, which stretched back in Wessex to the time of the Romans, was brought to its end with the onset of the First World War. With the great need for food crops many vineyards were 'grubbed out'. Sugar was in short supply and eventually rationed. People to do the labouring work were in even shorter supply. For the first time in nearly 2000 years English wines were no longer being produced in Wessex, nor the rest of the country.

Louis Pasteur 1822–1895   A MEAL WITHOUT WINE IS LIKE A DAY WITHOUT SUNSHINE

Vinegrowing in the region begins to develop

The dull image of English wine took hold during the thirty-year hiatus in production between the World Wars. As the Second World War was beginning to develop so there were rumblings in the recesses of potential English vineyards. The accumulated knowledge of 2000 years had disappeared in an instant. In 1936 George Ordish planted vines and systematically wrote about his findings. Vinegrowers in Wessex and the south of England were now on a voyage of re-discovery. Other pioneers followed after the war. Ray Barrington-Brock set up his own Viticultural Research Station, which the government consistently refused to take seriously. Jack Ward founded the Merrydown Company which later became a central location for the developing English wine industry. Edward Hyams planted vines in Kent and in the extreme western limits of Wessex at Ashburton in Devon. Each documented their findings. None of these, so far, though, was a commercial venture.

Commercial vines

Then, in south-east Wessex, Hambledon in Hampshire gained its second of three claims to English fame. In 1952 Major-General Sir Guy Salisbury-Jones, was encouraged to plant vines on a commercial basis. The chalky soil is very similar to that of the Champagne region of France, of which he had experience. The first sales were made in 1955. Hambledon's third claim to fame was in 1973 when the estate actually began exporting wine to France.

There was a huge amount of bureaucratic confusion over this because, of course, the Customs and Excise had no forms relating to such an unheard-of situation. Today, unfortunately, this pioneering vineyard is closed to the public, but throughout Wessex other vineyards are flourishing and welcoming visitors. (Oh, yes, and the first famous association made with Hambledon? It's regarded as the home of something with a far shorter history than English wine. The game of cricket started here.)

'If the weather does not improve, this will be our last season.'

The second commercial vineyard in this period of renaissance was planted in 1960 in the same corner of Wessex. It was the work of Colonel and Mrs Gore Brown at Beaulieu, where they planted five acres of vines.

Now a whole new body of relevant information was being drawn together that had particular reference to the situation in England, as opposed to, say, that in France or Germany. The enthusiasts could compare notes on soils, grape types, climate and growing techniques. The must of English wine was really beginning to flow again. Thus in 1967 Sir Guy and Jack Ward founded the English Vineyards Association. (This has now been superceded by the UK Vineyards Association and affiliated Regional Associations – details at the end of the book.) In 1969 Jack Ward offered vinegrowers 'co-operative' facilities at his own farm. This enabled growers who could not afford a winery to bring their grapes to him for processing, and so make the wine that was, after all, the objective of all their hard work.

Meanwhile, a mere 24 years later, in 1970, the Government's Ministry of Agriculture began to realise that Ray Barrington-Brock's research could be of importance after all. This was just as, in old age, he had closed down his own self-funded Research Station. So they continued his work at their research centre in north-west Wessex at Long Ashton, just outside Bristol.

By 1974, 40 commercial vineyards had registered themselves with the EVA, as well as over 300 non-commercial vineyards. English wine was gaining a very good reputation. In 1978, a blind tasting was held at Christies and many English wines were placed above French and German ones. In the same year, the Pilton Manor Vineyard, in the Wessex county of Somerset, exported its wine to Northern Italy. Now the wheel of 2000 years of English winemaking had really turned full circle.

The seasons dominate our vineyard life and the harvest is the culmination of our year's work. Friends gather to pick the grape harvest and take the crop to the winery in our 1930s lorry. We then enjoy the fruits of the previous year's harvest with an accompanying lunch – the experience is always leisurely and full of flavour – rather like a good wine!

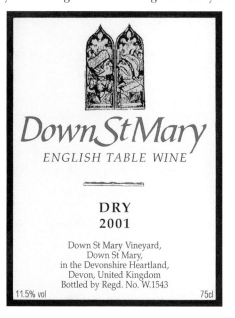

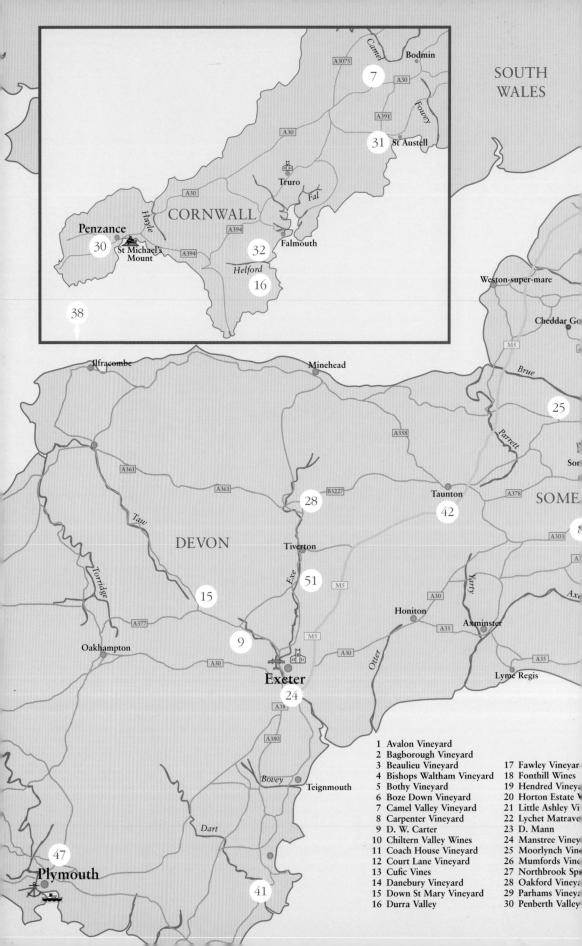

SOUTH
WALES

CORNWALL

Penzance
St Michael's
Mount

Truro

Falmouth

Helford

Bodmin

St Austell

7

31

30

32

16

38

Weston-super-mare

Cheddar Go

Ilfracombe

Minehead

Brue

25

Parrett

A358

Taunton

42

SOME

DEVON

28

Tiverton

51

Sor

A378

A303

8

A

15

Honiton

Axminster

Axe

9

Oakhampton

Exeter

24

Lyme Regis

Teignmouth

Plymouth

47

41

1 Avalon Vineyard
2 Bagborough Vineyard
3 Beaulieu Vineyard
4 Bishops Waltham Vineyard
5 Bothy Vineyard
6 Boze Down Vineyard
7 Camel Valley Vineyard
8 Carpenter Vineyard
9 D. W. Carter
10 Chiltern Valley Wines
11 Coach House Vineyard
12 Court Lane Vineyard
13 Cufic Vines
14 Danebury Vineyard
15 Down St Mary Vineyard
16 Durra Valley

17 Fawley Vineyar
18 Fonthill Wines
19 Hendred Vineya
20 Horton Estate V
21 Little Ashley Vi
22 Lychet Matrave
23 D. Mann
24 Manstree Viney
25 Moorlynch Vine
26 Mumfords Vine
27 Northbrook Spr
28 Oakford Vineya
29 Parhams Vineya
30 Penberth Valley

43

Oxford

OXFORDSHIRE

A46
A417
A429

Cirencester

A419

GLOUCESTERSHIRE

A338

Abingdon **5**

19

10

M5

Malmesbury

A419   A420

Wantage

17

A429

M4

Swindon

Uffington
(White Horse)

45

BERKSHIRE

6

Chippenham

Calne

Windmill Hill

A345

Marlborough

Reading

A4

Silbury
Hill

Avebury
(Stone Circle)

Savernake

Hungerford

Newbury

35

Bath   **26**

A4

A342

Devizes

A346

A338

A4

A343

Bradford-on-Avon

21

Trowbridge

WILTSHIRE

A342

Basingstoke

A361

A350

Westbury

A338

Andover

Test

49

A34

M3

Frome

1

pton Mallet

Warminster

A360

Test

A30

33

2

50

Wylye

A338

A272

A31

A359

Hindon

18

Wilton

Stonehenge
(Prehistoric Site)

A30

Winchester

12

A303

A350

Salisbury

Itchen

14

Winchester

h Cadbury

Shaftesbury

A30

29

23

A30

Rockbourne

Romsey

M3

Hamble

Sherborne

A350

A354

Cranborne

HAMPSHIRE

11

27

Southampton

Meon

4

e Abbas
Giant

Blandford Forum

20

Ringwood

Beaulieu

A31

48

46

DORSET

A354

Wimborne
Minster

A31

3

44

Portsmouth

Dorchester

Piddle

22

Poole

40

Maiden
Castle

Frome

Wareham

37   Isle of Wight   **36**

Weymouth

Swanage

34

Portland Bill

♔	Capitals of Wessex
⚱	Royal burial sites
▥	Roman sites
⊛	Railway centre
⚓	Naval ports
⬚	Trading ports

Champion English Wines

Thomas Love Peacock
1785–1866

THE JUICE OF THE GRAPE IS THE LIQUID QUINTESSENCE OF CONCENTRATED SUNBEAMS

English wines were riding high. The momentum increased. In August of 1979, a white wine from Shepton Mallet, Somerset, was the easy winner in a tasting of wines from seven countries held in Moselle. In that same year a 1978 wine of the Wootton Vineyard, Somerset, beat all the French and German châteaux wines in the Traminer Wine Olympiad. This was from a vineyard of only three acres.

Government favours foreign wines

The battle for Government recognition still continued. The Ministry refused to count winemaking as part of agriculture, as it was in France and Germany, and thus levied huge taxes (£1.40 per bottle). This meant that wine from France and Germany could be bought more cheaply in England than English wine. Government Ministries have never been renowned for their grasp of reality. The Wessex winemakers accepted their lot stoically, kept up their lobbying and kept on producing good wines.

English wines travel abroad

Today English, and Wessex, wines are being exported as far afield as China and Japan. A reverse Beaujolais Nouveau race was started by taking an English Beaujolais to Paris. The wines are found in the Houses of Parliament, top class and other hotels, supermarkets, Harrods and British Airways.

New vineyards

Wessex is at the heart of the renaissance of English winemaking. The medieval Church domains of Wessex, such as Winchester, Salisbury, Sherborne, Dorchester, Wells, Bath, Bristol and Exeter, do not have the same vineyards as in those times. But the new vineyards are now sprouting

ENGLISH TABLE WINE
PRODUCED AND BOTTLED AT
SETLEY RIDGE
VINEYARD
LYMINGTON ROAD
BROCKENHURST
HAMPSHIRE SO42 7UF
TELEPHONE 01590 622 246
SETLEY.RIDGE@AMSERVE.NET
10.5% Vol 75cl ℮ PRODUCE OF THE UK

SETLEY RIDGE
WINE FROM THE NEW FOREST
1999 DRY WHITE LEES AGED WINE

TREES OF THE NEW FOREST
—— SILVER BIRCH ——

on a sound scientific and often commercial basis. King Alfred can rest easy. The revels and customs of the Saxon 'Wyn Moneth' still exist, 1000 years on, in his former kingdom, Wessex.

First let's be clear on the difference between a vineyard and winery. The vineyard is where grapes are grown. The winery is where the grapes are manufactured into wine. A large vineyard will often also have its own winery. Small vineyards may well have to send their grapes to a winery for pressing and other processes if they do not have enough grapes or capital to be able to manage the expense of setting up their own equipment. The wine produced is still their own but cannot be claimed as estate made. This is not quite the same as, say, a cooperative in France which keeps and then blends the wines brought in from its local area. It is more akin to the way, in the Middle Ages, the small cereal-crop farmers would take their grain to the local miller for grinding, collect it again in sacks and take it separately from another farmer's flour if they wanted to sell it as their own.

Vineyard or winery?

The vines need as much sunshine as the climate will allow. Thus south and south-west facing slopes are favoured. Poor and well-drained soils are good for the vines since they benefit from having to work for a living. If the soil is too rich and moist, which the vines love, they put all their energy into growing everything except grapes. International laws can prevent watering of the vines but, in Britain, this is seldom necessary.

What vines need

White wine grapes well-suited to Wessex and Britain

Huxelrebe – A German vine with a distinctive muscat flavour.

Kerner – A modern breed from the classic Riesling grape. A late ripener at the end of October.

Madeleine Angevine – A vine capable of delivering a good crop in poor summers, and which is relatively new to Britain.

Muller Thurgau – A German vine, one of the most popular in the vineyards of Wessex and Britain as a whole.

Regner – This is a new variety of vine. A cross between the French Gamay and an Italian vine.

Reichsteiner – A popular and reliable German vine.

Schonburger – A new vine developed in Germany.

Seyval Blanc – Originally a hybrid French developed vine, it is now grown widely here, the Loire and the the United States. It is very resistant to diseases.

Red wine grapes most likely to be found

Pinot Noir – The classic French grape.

Triomphe – An Alsace grape gaining in popularity as a reliable source of red wine in Wessex and Britain.

Which Grape on Which Trellis?

WINE IS BOTTLED POETRY

Most vineyards grow a variety of grapes. With the industry still being relatively new, experimentation continues. Having a mixture of grape varieties means that in a good season wines can be made from single grape types, and in poor seasons good blends can be achieved. Furthermore, the different varieties will not all ripen at the same time. This helps spread the workload.

Since most vines grown in Wessex are white grape types they can be best distinguished by their differences in leaf shape. Before leaves have emerged, though, even the proprietors will need to consult their planting schedules to be sure which is which.

There are three main systems used in Wessex for supporting the vines. These are: Geneva Double Curtain, Double Guyot and Bordeaux Lyre Trellis. Essentially the trellis is there to keep the vine supported above the ground. This is important in several considerations: to allowing easy pruning; to allow easy picking; to support sufficient leaf cover. The site may be easily attacked by frost so the height above ground, say in a low valley, will be important too. Thus the trellis will keep the new buds out of the reach of the frost.

Two further aspects of the choice of trellises are, the cost of installing and maintaining them and the time taken for the vine to reach the trellis, spreading and then produce the grapes. For instance, vines on the lower Double Guyot will take three or four years to spread, but on the higher Geneva system the wait may be as long as six to seven years. When you consider that setting up a vineyard can cost around £5,000 per acre, then waiting for seven years before you even begin to see some returns

FURLONG

2000

Madeleine Angevine

Seyval Blanc

English Table Wine

PRODUCED BY HENDRED VINEYARD
IN THE VALE OF WHITE HORSE, OXFORDSHIRE, U.K.

75 cl   Produce of the United Kingdom   11% vol

ENGLISH TABLE WINE
Wickham Vineyard is an 18 acre estate on a sheltered south facing slope in Hampshire. The grapes are harvested by hand in the traditional way during October each year.

Produced by Wickham Vineyard
Shedfield, Hampshire, UK
Telephone 01329 834042

75cle 12.0%vol
PRODUCE OF THE UK

ESTATE BOTTLED

WICKHAM

Special Release

2000

Fumé
DRY

Wickham Fumé is produced mainly from Bacchus and Reichensteiner grapes. It has been fermented and matured in new French oak barrels. Great care has been taken not to over oak the wine, and the result is a fine balance of fruit and oak that makes superb drinking on its own, or a perfect accompaniment to fish or white meat dishes, or with cheese.

Angela Baart
WINEMAKER

could stretch purse strings to the limit. And that cost is after you have bought the land.

Winter and early spring: Pruning throughout this period encourages the vine to grow strong, thereby yielding a good harvest of grapes.

March–April: Buds appear. Followed by flowering.

May–June: Berries set and grapes are on their slow path to maturity. The acidic juices in the grape gradually turn to sugar. The leaves are instrumental in this metamorphosis. The amount of sugar determines the initial alcohol content and the quality of the wine.

September–November: October, remember, was the Saxon 'Wyn Moneth' for grape harvesting. First allow the dew (or rain) to evaporate. The grapes are cut and gathered in whole bunches. Then they are transported to the Winery. A busy time but a time laden with expectation.

Camel Valley is Cornwall's largest vineyard, situated on the sunny slopes above the River Camel, halfway between the Atlantic and the Channel coasts. Traditional vineyard practices combined with a New World approach to wine making ensure high quality red, white and sparkling wines. Camel Valley wines have won many prestigious National and International awards.

Sparkling wines were made in England as long ago as 1660.
On 17 December 1662, Englishman Christopher Merret presented a paper to the Royal Society on how to 'render wines sparkling' – more than 30 years before the French made their first sparkling Champagne! Camel Valley Sparkling Wine is bottle fermented and rendered sparkling using the 'traditional Merret method' of 1662.

Bob Lindo
Wine maker

A Twelvemonth in the Vineyard

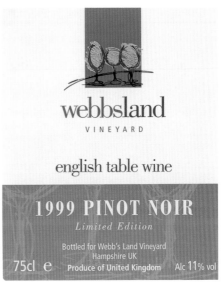

Work in the Winery

John Clarke c. 1650   WINE MAKES OLD WIVES WENCHES

Many people are surprised to find that almost all grape juice is white or colourless, in fact. Try it. Take a red grape and squeeze it onto a white plate. It is clear. So, how do we get red and rosé wine then? The longer the squeezed juice is left in contact with the red skins the darker it becomes. (Only a couple of grape varieties actually have red juice and most countries do not allow their use, so that the customer cannot be deceived into thinking it is an authentic red wine.) Thus the different reds are the result of the creativity of the estate. Of course there is more to it than that. But that is the essence of it. The estate must weigh up the amount of colour against the amount of tannin and acid desired for the flavour of the particular wine. Red wines will not need extra tannin so they will be de-stalked. If white wines need more tannin they will have the stalks left on them.

Another surprising thing about the winery is that it contains lots of stainless steel vessels and machinery as opposed to the often expected wood. Winemaking has moved with the times.

The range of tasks carried out in the winery will depend upon the size (and therefore the available capital) of the estate. However, in a fully

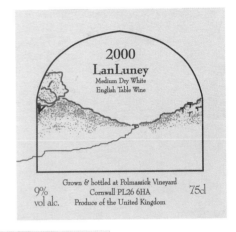

operational winery the following tasks will be undertaken: pressing (to produce the 'must'), filtering, fermentation (left to work through the winter and spring), clearing the wine by 'racking' it off to leave the sediment (or 'lees') behind and also 'fining' it further if necessary; bottling, corking and packaging. Naturally, during the early stages in the winery, testing is done to check tannin, acidity and sugar levels. The estate has to decide when to move onto the next step of the process.

Dry wine is the easiest to produce. In this case nearly all the sugar has been converted to alcohol during fermentation. Sweeter wines are made either by stopping the fermentation at a desired point or by adding unfermented sweet grape juice once fermentation has stopped. The latter method is easier to control to give the desired sweetness. Changes of temperature are not good for the wine and sunlight will leech its colour, so the finished bottles are best kept, literally, in the dark.

British and *English* wines are not the same product by any means. *British wine* is made from imported grape juice concentrates and has largely been discontinued. It is also what gave our wine its bad name in modern times. *English wine* is made from grapes grown in England.

From 'must' to packaging

Beenleigh Manor Vineyards are part of the Sharpham Partnership featured below.

xceptional sweet wine
a zesty orange character,
ginta Nobilis is produced
late, hand-harvested
elrebe grapes affected by
'Noble Rot' and trodden in
vat. Indulgent yet light on
palate Nobilis will drink
utifully now or age
derfully. Serve chilled.

RPHAM PARTNERSHIP,
ES, SOUTH DEVON, U.K. TQ9 7UT
.sharpham.com

SHARPHAM
Octoginta Nobilis
ENGLISH TABLE WINE

10.5% vol.   PRODUCE OF THE U.K.   25cl. e

OCTOGINTA NOBILIS
Meaning 'noble eighty' this
wine is dedicated to our
founder Maurice Ash who
participated in the grape
picking on his eightieth
birthday. This superb and
extremely rare English wine
is produced from botrytised
grapes from the '97,
'98 & '99 vintages.

Bottle No. _____ of 1966

THE SHARPHAM VINEYARD · TOTNES · SOUTH DEVON

Artistry on the Wine Bottle

Three Choirs Vineyard was one of the first large commercial vineyards to be planted in the UK and over the last 25 years has established itself as a major force in English wine. It is by far the largest and most important vineyard in the western half of the UK and makes wines under contract for many growers.

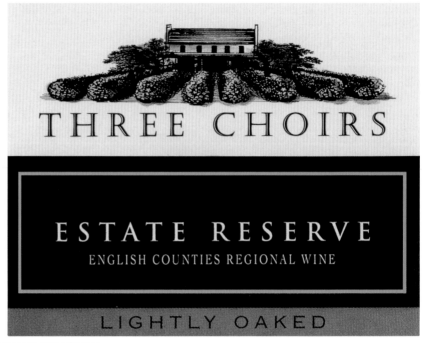

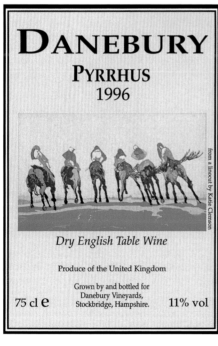

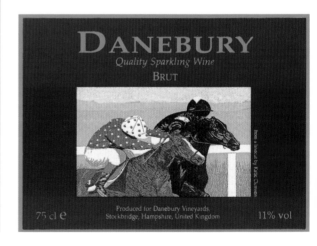

Titchfield

1999
FUMÉ
English Table Wine

Estate Grown & Bottled By
C.A. & N.A. Baker, Titchfield Vineyard,
Hampshire, U.K.

11.5%vol   75cl℮

St. Martin's

Vineyard

Isles of Scilly

FOR A BRAND
NEW EXPERIENCE
IN THE ISLANDS

SEE A WORKING
VINEYARD IN ACTION

First Vintage 2000

2000
Carnival
English Table Wine
Estate Grown & Bottled By
11%vol   C.A. & N.A. Baker, Titchfield Vineyard, Hampshire, U.K.   75cl℮

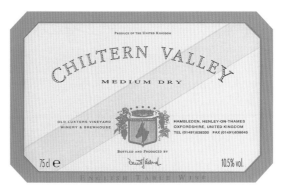

PRODUCE OF THE UNITED KINGDOM

CHILTERN VALLEY
MEDIUM DRY

OLD LUXTERS VINEYARD
WINERY & BREWHOUSE

HAMBLEDEN, HENLEY-ON-THAMES
OXFORDSHIRE, UNITED KINGDOM
TEL (01491)638330 FAX (01491)638645

BOTTLED AND PRODUCED BY

75 cl ℮   10.5% vol.

ENGLISH TABLE WINE

GAZETTEER

BERKSHIRE

Rock's Country Wines
Loddon Park Farm, Twyford
Valley Vineyards
Stanlake Park, Twyford, Reading RG10 0BN
Tel: 0118 934 0176

CORNWALL

Camel Valley Vineyard
Little Denby Farm, Nanstallon, Bodmin PL30 5LG
Tel: 01208 77959
Trevor Lockwood
Durra Valley, Maraccar, Helston
Private, no sales, but produces wine
Penberth Valley Vineyards
St Buryan, Penzance TR19 6HH
Tel: 01736 810714 Fax: 01736 810714
Wine sales and visits by appointment only
Polmassick Vineyard
Polmassick St Ewe, St Austell, Cornwall
PL26 6HA
Tel: 01726 842239 Fax: 01726 842239
Porthallow Vineyard
Porthallow Road, St Keverne, Helston TR12 6QH
Tel: 01326 280050
St Martin's Vineyard
Isles of Scilly. *Address for correspondence*: 'Greystokes',
Beach Road, Heybrook Bay, Plymouth PL9 0BS
Tel: 01752 862019

DEVON

D. W. Carter
Rock Moors, Woodland Head, Crediton EX17 5HE
Down St Mary Vineyard
The Old Mill, Down St Mary, Nr Crediton
EX17 6EE
Manstree Vineyard
New Barn Farm, Manstree Road, Shillingford St
George, Exeter EX2 9QR
Tel: 01392 832218 Fax: 01392 832747
Oakford Vineyard
The Old Rectory, Holme Place, Oakford, Bampton
EX16 9EW
Tel: 01398 351486
Sharpham Vineyard
Sharpham Estate, Ashprington, Totnes TQ9 7UT
Tel: 01803 732203 Fax: 01803 732122
Weir Quay
Bere Alston, Yelverton

Yearlstone Vineyard
Bickleigh EX16 8RL
Tel: 01884 855700 Fax: 01844 855726

DORSET

Horton Estate Vineyard
Horton, Wimborne, BH21 7JG
Tel: 01258 840258/480990
Lychet Matravers Vineyard
Poole, BH16 6HP
Tel: 01929 459526
Parhams Vineyard
Parhams Farm, Melbury Abbas, Shaftesbury, SP7 0DE
Tel/Fax: 01747 853122
Purbeck Vineyard
Valley Road, Harmans Cross, Corfe Castle, BH20 5HU
Tel: 01929 481525

GLOUCESTERSHIRE

Three Choirs Vineyard
Newent GL18 1LS
Tel: 01531 890555   Office: 01531 590223
Shop/Restaurant Fax: 01531 890877
Saint Augustine's Vineyard
The Old Parsonage, Aust BS35 4BG
Tel: 01454 632236 Fax: 01454 632236

HAMPSHIRE

Beaulieu Vineyard
John Montague Building, Brockenhurst, Beaulieu
SO42 7ZN
Tel: 01590 612345 Fax: 01590 612624
Bishops Waltham Vineyard
Tangier Lane, Bishops Waltham, Southampton
SO32 1BU
Tel: 01489 895803 Fax: 01489 893184
Wine sales and visits by appointment
Coach House Vineyard
Romsey
Tel: 01794 323345
Court Lane Vineyard
Ropley, Arlesford, SO24 0OE
Tel: 01962 773391
Danebury Vineyard
Danebury House, Nether Wallop, Stockbridge
SO20 6JX
Tel: 01264 781851 Fax: 01264 782212
Wine sales and visits by appointment

GAZETTEER

Northbrook Springs Vineyard
Beeches Hill, Bishop's Waltham, Southampton SO3 2IFB
Tel: 01489 892659

Prior's Dean Vineyard
Alton, Petersfield.
Correspondence to: 5 St Mary's Road, Liss GU3 7AN

Setley Ridge Vineyard
Lymington Road, Setley, Brockenhurst
SO42 7UF
Tel: 01590 622246

Titchfield Vineyard
Misty Haze, Brownwich Lane, Titchfield PO14 6NZ.

Webbsland Vineyard
Webbsland, Tanfield Lane, Wickham, PO17 5NS
Tel: 01329 833633   Fax: 01329 834600

Wooldings Vineyard
Wooldings, Whitchurch, RG28 7QT

Wickham Vineyard
Botley Road, Shedfield, Southampton SO32 2HL
Tel: 01329 834042   Fax: 01329 834907

ISLE OF WIGHT

Rosemary Vineyard
Rosemary Lane, Ryde PO33 8UX
Tel: 01983 811084

Rossiter's Vineyard
Wellow, Yarmouth PO41 0TE
Tel: 01983 761138

OXFORDSHIRE

Bothy Vineyard
Frilford Heath, Abingdon. *Address for correspondence:*
Amphora, Crays Pond, Reading RG8 7QJ
Tel: 01491 681484

Boze Down Vineyard
Hardwick Road, Whitchurch-on-Thames,
Reading TG8 7QS

Chiltern Valley Wines
Old Luxters Vineyard, Hambleden,
Henley-on-Thames RG9 6JW
Tel: 01491 638330

Fawley Vineyard
The Old Forge, Fawley Green, Henley-on-Thames
RG9 6JA
Tel: 01491 577998

Hendred Vineyard
Sheephouse Barn, Ludbridge, East Hendred
OX12 8HR

SOMERSET

Avalon Vineyard
The Drove, East Pennard, Shepton Mallet, BA4 6UA
Tel: 01749 860393

Bagborough Vineyard
Pylle, Shepton Mallet BA4 6SX
Tel: 01747 831146   Fax: 01749 830832

Carpenter Vineyard
Norton sub Hamdon TA14 6SN
Tel: 01935 881255

Cufic Vines
Cheddar

Moorlynch Vineyard
Bridgewater TA7 9DD
Tel: 01458 210393

Mumfords Vineyard
Shockerwick Lane, Bannerdown, Bath
BA1 7LQ
Tel: 01225 858367   Fax: 01225 852385

Staplecombe Vineyard
Burlands Farm, Staple Grove, Taunton, TA2 6SN
Tel: 01823 451217   Fax: 01823 451726

WILTSHIRE

Little Ashley Vineyard
Bradford-on-Avon BA15 2AL
Tel: 01225 866917   Fax: 01225 866114

Fonthill Wines
The Winery, Teffont, Salisbury
Tel: 01722 716770

D. Mann
Vineyard House, Bowerchalke, Salisbury
SP5 5BE
Sells grapes to other vineyards

Wylye Valley Vineyard
Crockerton, Warminster, Wiltshire
Correspondence to: Mill Farm House, Hill Deverill
BA12 7EF
Tel: 01985 211337   Fax: 01985 841066

This Gazetteer is not exhaustive but is as accurate as we
could make it from the information supplied to us.
Please advise us if we have wrongly omitted or included
any vineyard.

Charles Dickens 1812–70   BRING IN THE BOTTLED LIGHTNING, A CLEAN TUMBLER, AND A
CORKSCREW

So, what is it really like to set up a vineyard in Wessex, this ancient area of England's winemaking? Great energy, enthusiasm and optimism are obviously a minimum requirement. Paul Dale planted his Wylye Valley Vineyard in 1989 on the higher valley sides of the upper reaches of the Wylye River. This Wessex stream snakes its way eastwards, down through picturesque villages, through Wilton, the ancient capital of Wessex – whose name and that of the county, Wiltshire, both derive from it – and finally on to merge with the River Avon at Salisbury.

The site was chosen for several reasons. The valley offers a warm microclimate by being sheltered. The greensand soil drains well. Choosing the higher slopes means that the vines should avoid any frosts which tend to keep to the valley floor.

Nine acres were planted in 1989 using approximately 6,000 vines. Three varieties were used: two French (Regner and Seyval Blanc) and one German (Kernling). The vines were then not allowed to bear grapes until their third year, making them much stronger and able to hold a fully ripe crop.

The buds will burst at the end of April or the beginning of May. The short two-week flowering period occurs around the first week of July. Vine flowers are not particularly impressive, but this short period is vital. Good weather during the flowering determines the size of the crop.

A delicate balance now has to be kept with the aid of judicious pruning and application of fertiliser. If you allow the vine to grow too strongly too little fruit will result. But leaves, also, are vital. Too few and the grapes will not ripen well because it is the leaves which put the sugar into the grapes. The leaves will be removed later, in the full summer, to allow sunlight to reach the grapes which will enhance their colour and flavour. Also trimming the leaves allows air to circulate and lessen the likelihood of disease.

The three varieties ripen at different times allowing the gathering to be spread throughout the month of October. Pruning begins in November and will take one person around two or three months. If pruning is done when frost is threatened the cut will not heal and the vine may be severely damaged.

Spraying is done to counter diseases such as mildew and botrytis. One advantage of vinegrowing in England, compared to, say, France, is that the insects which feed on the vines have not yet established themselves. The phylloxera louse that has done so much damage in the past likes vine roots. However, as it does not like American vine roots, the Wylye Valley Vineyard has followed the course taken throughout Europe and grafted its vines onto American roots.

Currently the vineyard's average production is 22 tonnes of grapes, giving about 18,000 bottles. This means that each vine produces about three bottles.

For the three previous years the grapes were sold to other vineyards, but in 1994 the grapes were made into wine by a Welsh vineyard. One of the wines was awarded a silver medal in the 1995 English Wine of the Year Competition, in which 117 wines were entered.

The River Wylye, cruising past at the bottom of the vineyard, is well-known for fly fishing. Hence, Wylye Valley Vineyard wine labels have illustrations of fishing flies on them.

England has advantages over France

> ### THE PURBECK VINEYARD
>
> Vineyards are constantly coming into production, and 'Purbeck' at Corfe Castle will sell wine in 2003. There were vineyards here in Roman times, on the northern end of the Kimmeridgean shale which runs down past Chablis . . .

Vineyard Associations

IN OCTOBER DRINK NEW WINE AND EAT MINNOWS

The United Kingdom Vineyards Association (UKVA) was formed in 1996 to take over from the English Vineyards Association (EVA).

The six eligible regional associations have all now affiliated to the UKVA. They are:

The South West Vineyards Association

The Wessex Vineyards Association

The South East Vineyards Association

The Thames and Chilterns Vineyards Association

The Mercian Vineyard Association

The East Anglian Wine Growers Association

The UKVA organizes meetings for members – the annual conference and the Vintners' Symposium – publishes the *Grape Press*, runs the annual Wine of the Year Competition and the House of Lords prizegiving, operates the Quality and Regional Wine Schemes, liaises with members of the public, wine trade and media who want information about English and Welsh wine, arranges tastings, organizes council meetings and meetings with DEFRA, Customs and Excise and the Wine Standards Board.

For comprehensive information on wines, growers, types of grape and anything else that needs to be known about the vineyards and wines of England, Wales, Ireland and the Channel Isles, Stephen Skelton's book *The Wines of Britain and Ireland*, published by Faber and Faber should be consulted. Stephen Skelton is the current chairman of the UKVA.